Dancing
on
Occam's Razor

by

Andrew Amster

Smudgeworks Press
Framingham, Massachusetts

Selected poems have previously appeared in *Midway Review, Winewood Journal, Mountain Thought Review, Poetalk, Black Buzzard Review, Raw Dog, New Mexico Humanities Review, Buckle, Parting Gifts, Crazyquilt, Clock Radio, Wind,* and *Woodstock Poetry Review.*

Smudgeworks Press
6 Bancroft Circle
Framingham, MA 01701

You may contact the writer at:
andrew@smudgeworks.com

Cover photo & design by Andrew Amster

ISBN-13: 978-0-9864426-0-5

Dedicated to the late
Maxine Cassin
and
Everette Maddox.
Your New Orleans is the possum
singing inside my head.

Contents

Passing for Adulthood

Dancing
on
Occam's Razor

Spring Poem

It's spring again.
Birds stop at the feeder and move on.
A chipmunk stays and digs deeper.
Trees are bursting with sudden green.
Nature is, all at once,
both fecund and voracious.
Things blossom
where last week there was no bud.
Things frozen since Halloween
thaw and quickly rot.
And all these things with feathers?
They suddenly need to fuck and nest
and give birth to next year's tweety fuckers.
Nature is nothing if not
simple and elegant,
predictably precise.
Over time, spring will give way to summer
like the winding down of a clock.
(I admit that analogy is an anachronism.
I am surrounded by clocks with no springs to wind,
no keys with which to do the winding.)

Why is it that spring makes me feel so old?
Why should each goldfinch smack down
make me ponder brevity, certainty,
gravity, and the perils of forgetting one's own spring
     folly?

You remember spring folly?
She was a kiss on the bus
of an April fieldtrip.
She was a May one night stand
and more than one June goodbye.
My god, I've been gloriously stupid.

On this downward path, I've seen it all
more times than I'll see it again.
And that's that. *Fait accompli.*
There's no arguing with the hammer
when you're a nail.

And that's OK. It's good. I'm fine.
Despite how it sounds,
I am not wistful.
I am not mournful.
I am in love and my cock still works
(like me, in fits and starts).
I am awake and aware and often amused
(tall but shrinking, wise if sanguine).
And I am full of both speculation
and more than an occasional pumpkin ale.

Life recedes and I accede.
Decades. I have decades to watch these birds.

Clueless Youth
1975 to 1982

Ho-Ho and Rice Cake
Across the Crowded Room

The party is a crockpot creation —
people thrown together and simmered whole,
pot roast and pearl onions,
freshmen, a keg, a professor's wife
in blue angora, leaning close.
Peas couple with beans
and the potatoes are all over the carrots
in someone's parents' room.

You're killing me slowly, you know,
with these hungry looks, your eyes wide,
sizing-up, nibbling, devouring on the spot,
followed too quickly by some shudder of regret,
reining in, looking away —
this need of yours to purge before a single bite is taken.

I'm spoiling too quickly in the heat of neglect,
stumped by those, like you, on an emotional diet.

I won't sacrifice another calorie of my attention
to your ambivalent binges, the double-talk
and double standards. I cannot waste flirtations
on your unfillable emptiness and projectile posturing.

Screw your potential disappointment.
I'm not that guy. You're not that onion.

In My Efficiency

My apartment rug
is a blue battlefield, splotched
and spotted like a childhood disease —
ink spots (not mine),
food spots (mostly not mine),
spots that move and have to be stepped on,
pencil shavings, nomadic dustballs
that travel in hairy groups,
letters read, books unopened,
an apple, and an empty bottle of wine.
And floating above, hiding beneath,
everywhere white on blue...
are feathers —
sinister and sneaky,
perhaps silently spawning,
that I nightly sleeping
pull from my pillow.
Piling up, I presume
they are much like me —
all of us, confined and claustrophobic,
rolling from bed to wall and back,
doing nothing if not
seriously seeking life
a lot less cluttered.

Encounters with an Idol

Just once I'd like to meet you
when I'm bathed and groomed,
handsome, dashing,
charming, witty,
and brilliant as pearl.

Or barring the return
of Moses and miracles,

just bathed.

Ode to Pangaea

Oh, ye massive slice of land,
perhaps you thought yourself too grand,
and as result of inflated ego,
your pieces now across the sea go.
Pangaea, don't think that I'm a cynic,
if I call you schizophrenic.

Lethargy

Man and myth —
still waters, all that deep
movement fro and to.
We sleep in, unmotivated
by any better-invented
dragon.

Under a Waxen Sun

Cluelessly bobbing for apples
in a pail of beach plums,
feeling for mangoes
in a box of desert pears,
my soft scrabbling fingers
have edged sideways into unexpected sand.

Miss Muldaur, why is your oasis dry?
I swear, I followed the map.
I crept past angled ventifacts.
I rubbed your rounded belly dune
and slipped down past hidden palms.
My thirst is a question, your desire a mirage.

This analogy is as clumsy
as the act itself. Now the camels
are only going through the motions
of caring about their next drink.
The cacti have thrown up their arms in disgust.
It's time for me to fold up my tents.

If either of us sighs, the sound
is swallowed up by the Fleetwood Mac
throbbing from the room next door.
You don't bother to rebutton or zip.
You can go your own way, so you do.

I think, on a campus this size, surely
there must be another

cactus mouse in bed with
someone (sadly) not a mouse.

I can't be the only sucker
attempting cross-species foreplay.
But I am a mouse. I am *the* mouse.
I squeak and blow the candle out.

Between Beds

Walking home after midnight,
I see moths hurling overhead;
they weave white circles around streetlamps,
quietly tie them beaming to the black,
large stars among small, humming electric.

I smell of her,
the sweetness of her skin,
sourness of our fluid sex, turning,
no longer smelling of myself,
not really walking alone, wrapped in another.

The rhythm of footfall becomes smiling staccato.
A dog barks. My passing is witnessed after all.
Walking faster, I'm a thing drawn to the light,
one of us, or all of us, rising to the sky,
beginning to smell like darkness itself,
flying without purpose from star to star.

Someday I'll think of this as youth:
leaving one bed for another.

Love Gone by Like Little Deaths

kisses on the hand
nape of neck
toe ear small of spine
kisses in the wrong places
or at the wrong times
these are the kisses that itch
and tickle out of turn
these are the kisses like flies
things to be swatted
or simply rubbed away
two lips that kiss like foreign legs
two lips that brushed aside buzz back
and fly from skin to dung and back again

their nature is cotton and formaldehyde
kissing them is touching lips with zombies
lips that have no brains yet seek brains
lips that whisper memories of life
before flies and cotton and the itch

always the itch and the scratch
and the awkward morning partings
that won't affect our friendship
despite the cat's fisheye
the silence
the hug
and the itch

A Southern Scene

Emaciated girls
with babes
that howl as wolves,
your teenage faces
are drawn long
by little hands,
faster than the years.
Too soon your breasts
are gummed by the beardless
and are drawn long as well.
All this while
optional
husbands guzzle beer
unencumbered.

Nicholasville:
Before and After the Moon Died

Small town courthouse, city square,
Stone wall worn by weekend rumps,
elephantastic gold-painted tank
defends against attacking statues,
three bronze rebels, green sabers drawn,
riding horses with hot-pink balls.

All the same as before (months slip by),
the same as statues sleeping —
patina, wrinkles, drumming of rain.

A streetlight was installed
and no one noticed either
intrusion of change.

You, Me, and Boyle's Law

You remember that demonstration
where a mostly empty metal can
is heated, quickly sealed tight,
and placed in an ice-water bath?

For years (four years), we cycled
like alternating current, played like magnets:
plus to minus — clinging tightly, each to the other;
minus to minus — flying apart to studied silence.

Jeff kept saying we would outgrow
the hormone-induced delirium of our teens.
But how do I outgrow all these things
that stay with me like tattoos:

your blue eyes, the sound of your voice
in those umptillion hours of phonecalls,
the sat-through sock hops, movies,
water fights, notes, hayrides, tears —

that first holding-my-breath, circling kiss
or the afternoon you sat on my knee
and pulled off your green cat shirt?
Jeff was wrong. I've left my teens, but not you.

I can't regret first love, but the permanence
of its effect has left me hot and empty.
I'm tiring of these days when I can't help
sliding into the cold, again and again.

The can doubles over, collapses
on itself. It shrinks; it crumples.
The vacuum makes history of its form.
I always thought that was neat.

for Paula
Lexington
January, 1979

Life as a Tiring Drive

Looking back, I see
forked roads I never expected and
flat tires when there was no spare.
I see postcards I never sent
even when I had the right stamps.
I see my youth's enduring
predilection for wrong turns
even when directions were freely given.
I see a pile of maps folded the wrong way.

Apology: Colorado, 1979

Dead snake in the road,
white belly up,
curled into a letter G
spelling for God
who remembers Eden
and holds a grudge
like a '63 Corvair.

Donna: Second Meeting, First Date

"Jewish women…" — she pauses, smiling —
"…cannot fry chicken."

    I am sitting on unfamiliar wicker,
    waiting for the other shoe

"The batter won't stick."

    to drop.

"Something to drink?"

    I stare at the side of an iced tea glass
    and wonder how many pin-headed angels
    might backstroke there.
    The silence embraces the room
    like the smell of boiled cabbage.
    Stare, fumble.
    Perhaps the weather. Try that.

"It hasn't rained like this…"

    Her voice comes from her eyes,
    brightly darting,
    blinking, sea foam green.
    I've never seen eyes the color
    of eyes that color.

"…since Noah."

She knew him, I think.

"A Virgo," she says.

Of course, I sigh.
Aren't we all?

A Very Clever Imitation

The horseshoe, nailed to a tree, has slipped points down,
and all the luck's run out, rain and moon.

I believe in messianic things, self-evident,
pure and natural stigmata,
the decay of fruit, cobbles in streams.
I know where they go as I know where they've been —
the way stones rise from the field, they
float to the top of the earth without asking.

That time hiking up the creek to the falls,
we climbed over barbed wire, and she knew I saw
her cutoff's purple stain, a crooked red line
on her shaved white thigh.
She's mentioned it since, one side blushing,
the other daring me to deny it,
throwing it at me like a rock —
"So? I bleed!" —
waving the flag.
I've never doubted that, no.
I'm convinced of her humanity and yet...

We finally found my great-grandfather's marker,
high on a ridge, chipped and leaning.
The marble turned to powder when touched —
calcite white, moldy greens and grey.
We ate pears from the graveyard tree
and did a rubbing for her bedroom.

Only when the crayon pressed against the paper
did we see the palace and chiseled clouds.
And floating above this hard heaven, an all-seeing eye
like the back of a dollar-bill.

I learned of her first ten lovers
sitting on a rock in that dry creek bed.
Maybe nothing's proven by pear juice or blood.
Human is as human does, after all — bodies aside,
all those flat stones and no water for skipping —
wolf in sheep's clothing, android in drag.
Well-oiled, she'll never rust like that horseshoe.
No, not even that slow, cold fire for her —
black pool, distant Masonic eye.

You see, she never blinks.
That is, she never blinked for me.

New Orleans
1982 to 1986

The Night after the Day of the Semi-Annual Clearance Sale at Martin's Wine Cellar

The wine smells of piss and tastes of vinaigrette.
Pieces of cork cling to the glass, stuck in redolence.
It's after midnight, and I'm three drinks down
to a muse too fickle to fuck the landlord, that bitch.

Are those lizards? We're too far south for crickets,
and the roaches are too punked out on beer to chirp.
It's definitely a B-movie, flying saucer noise,
and I'm not pulling up those shades for no midnight rerun.

Two thousand miles away, you're drooling on the pillow
and dreaming that we all have more endearing qualities.
I don't know what you wear to bed when I'm not there…
something, I think, saving nothing for me, I hope.

It's after one, and the wine thinks I smell like lizards.
There's a toast on the edge of my glass, and I reach for you.

Giving All to What Is Present

The coot in the corner office is still spouting.
He's talked about it for days over coffee, talked until
his mustache droops, invectives melting wax.

"The whole damned world's gone nuts. Everybody's crazy
       as a newt.
Back twenty years ago, people didn't have time for…
Well, we were normal when *I* was a kid. It wasn't like this."

He learned his daughter's roommate dealt drugs, 'ludes in
       plush toys,
that another girl slit her wrists in the hall, "just two doors
       down."
He's shocked. Sipping coolly, we're surprised she
       died at all.

I have friends who anticipate the history he forgets.
They keep pills in case of war, tell me to cut with the grain.
Jaded, they know that classes go on and rugs are cleaned

and none of this strikes me as any more unusual
than ermine coats, bomb shelters, and freeze-dried food.
It wasn't like this before?

Not hard to imagine him, tongue-clucking at draft evaders.
Easier still to picture my great-grandfather, his brothers,
my name sneaking across eastern Europe to the sea.

He points to Moonies, but I see hopefuls stretched out,
shuffling in wide-eyed lockstep to the histrionics
of a Sister Aimee, a Smith, a Sabbatai-false-messiah

leading a line of empty pockets to some cliff of gold.
Can a man with dirty fingernails and a full trashcan
not have a few skeletons hanging about, clearing what
    pass for throats?

Didn't he have an aunt, dying of TB, who made
the children swear to pipe air to her coffin?
No lessons from black sheep or bastard cousins?

Crazy as a newt, we'll breathe water this year, air the next.
We'll put on our salamander skins and dance in fire.
We'll arrange lichens on his headstone, footnotes to
    forgetfulness.

We'll dance on Occam's razor.

Fast Food

They met at Schwegmann's
near the frozen fish and Cornish hens.
His cart was full of generic pasta;
she was buying green stuff and *Time*
        ("Read *Time* and you are there"—
            this week, a cover story on the new faith,
            and she *was* hopeful, if somewhat anemic).
Their wheels got locked like the braces
of this country's adolescent, orthodontic nightmares —
she spilled half and half on his shoe.
Later, they made love on the Scotchguard couch
while Dan Rather watched pointilistically
and the cats ate the last of the tassels,
licked his loafers clean.
When it was over, she cradled it like a wounded bird;
it fluttered, but never came back to the cage.

Reality set in sometime during *Family Feud*
as things thawing began to drip...
He asked her for a beer; she offered him her sandals
and a pamphlet on living better through tofu.
They traded recipes while they sorted clothes.
They gave away numbers like free samples
and kissed lightly at the door.

I'd like to say this was the beginning of something,
but he went home and ate pasta without meat sauce.
She pulled the shade and ate salad without dressing.

Hauntings by the Zeitgeist
(a poem in which the poet mourns
the loss of a diaphragm
and the woman who went with it)

Spreading onto stale toast the jam
made from last year's last berry —
the bread postdated, the flatware handed down,
the blue jam blue like the blue remembered
from a childhood night, staying,
and then having arrived, without thinking,
wearing in this heat yesterday's shirt,
last Sunday's magazine section read
on a streetcar built before this generation
became chemicals longing to become eggs.
Even the token was out of date,
turning up in change like an apparition,
too familiar for having never been seen.

My car forgets the familiar way to the airport;
only drugstore bags bring purple Concourse D to mind.

Last month's project covers the desk like shingles —
papers, erasable ink — progress to those who see it so.
What I see is a ball of twine with no ends,
a flightless bird, some opaque glass,
more than a few envelopes, sealed without stamps.
For the life of me, I don't know what to make
of you, agreeing to marry a stranger
as if you were still some dowry's sister,

living in the Pale, hiding from Cossacks,
milking cows in some tranquil Broadway dawn.
Our stories go their separate ways.
You'll have a canopy; I'll have a house with awnings.
And watching the Bosch paintings of the 6 o'clock news,
who's to say it's *not* best to put down the Wheaties,
the neon and soot — to blink and mosey back?

But I *like* neon, and the guys at
The Unity Universal Wings of Truth Church
said I could buy their sign cheap
when they have their "Second Coming Sale."

For that I'll wait. For you?
No more.

Like an apparition, there's corn starch in the kitchen,
bought for a piece of rubber no longer in the house.

Reconciliation

I can swallow no hopes of your return,
hear no echoes of madness, the buzzing
pleas of your voice on wings of steel,
mosquitos singing kamikaze lullabies
in the uneasy cave of a sleeping ear.
Your face hangs suspended like a fly
wrapped in a web, thinly covered, twitching
slightly, moving as if in a breeze.
In Capistrano, blue skies fill binoculars
like an accusation, a page not written on
by words on air, letters forgetting to return.

I've filled my tank at the Exxon a hundred times
without getting that eighth Libbey tumbler,
and they just don't make that pattern anymore,
seven glasses waiting on daisy shelf paper,
trying not to break for you, seven
then six, trying not to think of five,
of four, the fingers accidental tremble,
of three, your smile slipping to whimsy, to
two dusty glasses, waiting for just another
quick and painless
good-bye.

Sudden Long Distance Break-Up
(The Cabinet Trick)

Since last weekend's phone call ambush, I've been
bitter beyond the cure of pralines and puppies.
I admit I wallow. I roll in mourning like a dog in stink.
Nothing ventured. End of story. I don't know what I gained.

I guess it's lucky for you that we never married,
never lived together more than a week at a time,
never set a thing in stone or matching towels,
never allowed us to mean more to you than the space
I set aside for your clothes in my dresser drawers,
the toothpaste-sized gap in the medicine cabinet,
the water bottle for your morning runs —
I threw that away the following Tuesday
because it looked at me the wrong way.
These spaces were filled when you visited.
Now they echo with a decision I had no part in.

Upstairs, on this coast, an abandoned toothbrush
has become a monument to revisionism, a red plastic
ode of love and risk rewritten into passing acquaintance.
I imagine you're taking a more active approach where you are.
If I flew to L.A., I would find your journal entries
all whited out, all dog-ears turned to crisp newness.
Chosen parts of pages once written on
will have been erased, their truth redacted.
But those were real things, you know.
And what's been disappeared —
the lacuna, the least parts of the ink,

sweat, spit, semen, blood —
those were things that took up space,
things that noticed space,
things that still miss the things
that space once filled.
Things that are missing
are still things.

This look you won't allow is a pillar of Jello
on a base of clay, an untruth assuming no precedent
in countless looks, an unclenched fist
denying that it may have ever held
the damp and trembling fingers of another hand,
ever talked long into the night, cried in stereo,
ever meant enough to fight and not win.

You can hack the knot, take the shortest route,
spin magic from dross, turn it into paper fire
that bursts from nothing but empty sound.
You can gather the shards of broken china,
make them whole, pack them all over,
never stumble, never drop the box
on the way to the waiting truck,
never break what was never there.
You may as well try to juggle a sneeze.

Once I helped a laughing illusion
carry her boxes of cobwebs
into a house of cards
that we —for a while —
called home.

Despair Has Legs

i've lost whatever i had here.
it's gone, phfft — like that and smoke.
there is no — none, not at all —vapor,
but that's all past knowing,
microscopic in its corporeality,
like wrigglers in jism, motes in specks —
and maybe it's in the sun
(the Aztecs thought so, tails to sky)
or perhaps in the loo, belly up,
but it's vanished, you know, walked out,
and i only barely heard the tiffling
of its thousand untied shoes
and missed the good-byes altogether.
i'm not even sure i want it back,
whatever this was that deserted the nest.
let it find its own whatever it eats.
i was tired of picking up after it,
and never did know where it slept.
good riddance to you, you curmudgeon,
you phantom-color, smell-less "it" —
go, and take your atomic nightlight, and
the trophies, and your best friend, Friend
(whom i've always called Fear),
and slither, hop, or roll away from me —
no tears on either side.
where did i keep you, spot o'mine?
have i lost that, too? that as well?
what's that, spot? whut that?
this space for rent. so soon?

VA Hospital: Nurse on Rounds

Lily of the field, toe-tipping through the bedpans
to the sound of one man napping,
one man napping on eiderdown fluff,
dreaming of fluff and stuff and Lily

with her white stockings pulled down,
pulled off and giving him a sponge bath,
bathing him, bending over, wetting her hair,
using her hair to bathe him, damp and white,
white and damp white like Easter lilies.

Lily, so able,
she can turn him still asleep, change his sheets.
Lily, so able,
she can tuck his last good hope into his pajamas
without it bending, bowing good-bye.

We listen to the sound of one man dreaming,
of crepe soles slipping away on clean tile floors.

In this pause, the final shot is fired,
pale flower blooming on starched muslin,
daisy in the barrel of a guardsman's gun.

In flight, hope (for Jane)

"Friends," I thought,
kiss on the cheek,
or on the lips, quick and dry.
But we ("friends" I thought)
kiss on the mouth
for what seems like forever.

I see these two things in the sky.
They ascend. They plummet,
victims of inconstant wind,
the convergence of influences —
beach versus mountain,
ocean eddy versus chilly arctic whirl.

I think we're kites like they are,
except that we can't seem to soar.
We're grounded by logistics —
our art of annually being
the wrong version of us,
always the wrong place and time.

I kiss you and I'm a kite trying to fly,
the desire rising, gaining height
but whipped sideways without a tail.
You kiss me back, your kite
struggling with cable for cord
and our sighs an insufficient breeze.

In another field, one bright with sun
and the promises of thermals,
we could be gliders instead of kites —
the air rising to lift our weight,
us finally flying together
without all these strings.

What Was Once Clover Is Now Stop 43

They say it's winter in Australia.
They say it's evening at Neuchâtel.
They say time's a circle
  and the universe shaped much like a furrowed brow.

Morning...
Snake-eyed, I pass by, looking in windows
for signs of life: pinkly lit baths, yellow kitchens,
    a cracked refrigerator, taillights in the portico,
    sometimes a furtive robe at the front door,
    once, a ghostly, naked ass, hovering like dawn
    wielding a newspaper baton.
Here we are, all these oilmen, nurses, bums, maids —
in rows, we rock in wooden railway seats, nodding
as heat arcs white on the wires. Crackling,
it flashes color from thin, anemic sleep.
    Reluctantly, my heart pumps copious caffeine.

They say the streetcar is relaxing and quaint.
They say I'll have a window office by June.

Night...
Eyes wider but glazed, I see secretaries
walking in Nikes, driving by in foreign cars.
There's a man with no dentures, grinning wildly,
    selling the evening edition, making change in the rain.
    A man in a power tie gets splashed at the curb;
    a woman in a raincoat buys flowers for herself.

I sit in a car full of this day's strangers,
        looking for familiarity in the familiar, hitting
all the stops, pondering the purpose of Sanka,
push buttons, and the little holes in wingtip shoes.

They say I'll get a pension after 20 years.
They say the darkest hour
                is in the eye of a company man.

New Orleans
March, 1983

Poncho and Cisco at Taco Bell

Back booth — the Dean, chewing,
as nearby, refried beans harden
a greasy cheddar orange.
Lettuce, tomato, objects d'corn…
on this menu, all that is
is a la art.

Case in point: chile rellenos, green with cheese.
The Dean, uplooking from mental notes,
(complaints, budgets, sabbatical affairs)
a horn-rimmed blue-eyed seizure has.
The in-walking chiquita is pierced with
hot jalapeno hellos.

So it goes: she sits down, flat as a tortilla,
but with eyes like his, round as a picante "oh."
They touch beneath the table, two peppers
without roots, without limbs, with shoes.
Reaching for the same glass, their hands
are like mouths, burning with spice.

Three years now, they've lived with nerves
worn clean by Tabasco, yet dulled by beer.
He has a doctorate; she has a Selectric.
She types; he dictates over the phone.
They eat, talk, touch, stare, but to them
sex is still a mole best left untried.

Over fried ice cream, the Dean speaks ill of his wife.
She sighs; he sighs. Together, they eat ice cubes
and suck air like air conditioners, cooling down.

Across town, the Dean's wife is fucking the gardener
on Star Wars sheets taken from her son's room.
The secretary's cat has swallowed a bird from Ecuador
and run off to another neighborhood, looking for a drink…

margaritas in a bowl.

A French Legionnaire Caters the Last Oasis

saltation - *Geol.* a mode of sediment transport by which
particles jump, hop, bounce, or skip downwind or downstream.

His Woolco candles were guttering in the saucer
before that second glass of scotch splintered on their throats —
there was a pause big enough to swallow whole speeches
or sink inhibition. "Palpable," she might say.
She put on another Billie Holiday
and swished across the floor
like a sidewinder drunk on the blues.
When she said, "Let's dance,"
the ice melted in his drink, 'cause
them's the most baby-makin' words he knows.
They grab his gonads like pulsin', purple reins —
pull, stop on that one thin dime,
but the heavy breathing rider doesn't budge.
They wound 'round the furniture like snakes,
so close that clothes were thin as antique smoke,
so close they could feel each other's bumps and scales.
(Snakes have no hipbones, no small of back depression
where a rock once might have been,
not one thing round and shifting like the dunes.)
Later, she shed her dress in slick, dry ease.
She crawled on the bed, curled on warm asphalt, no headlights
in sight, arms rising as waves of heat shimmer up at noon.
And when he came to her, eggs were rolling
from between her legs
like small, wind-polished stones…

54

"Not yet, not yet," he whispered, pushing them back in,
dancing over her like silt in the storm, bouncing downwind.

Morning desire finds him filling her navel with salt
so that his next journey of a thousand miles
(or inches, forked tongues laid tip to tail)
can begin for thirst, end with rain.

An Absence of Intersection

Stuck in the pine sap of conversation,
a fly has chewed off its own wing
and bolted from this awkward arc toward amber.
What will we sacrifice when that fear sets in?

Or will we buy time with dinner table silences?
Whatever this is, it accumulates —
a thousand empty words that never blow away —
and yet we sit, up to our ears in the sediment.

It's too tight now, this fit of you on me.
I keep looking for a forked stick
on which to catch your splitting skin,
and peel it away, inside out.

When did we become parallel lines, you and I?
Why do we move in a dance of maintained distance,
always traveling in the same direction,
refusing to surrender a single point?

At least rays of light have hopes
of chance meet-ups with a convex lens —
a way to bend and not break,
a chance to turn toward, not away.

One Model, Representing Many

Between poses, the art class reels
back its dolorous eyeful,
blinks and stretches its legs.
The other students prowl the halls,
but Missy — the model — doesn't leave.
When you're naked, there's nowhere to go.
So she wanders the room, charcoal dust
sticking to her bare feet,
her robe clutched closed, walking
from easel to drawing board,
seeing herself reflected
in sketch after sketch —
different angles, views, styles.
All at once, here she stands,
the subject come to life.
And the subject wants to discuss my drawing:
my shading of her form;
the way I drew the irregular curve
of her calf, familiar to her, new to me.
The object is a subject is a person — is Missy —
telling me about that bruise I drew,
the table in the dark of her stairway
and the fucking corner that caught.
Her fingers on the edge of my pad,
inches from the sketch of her curled hand,
the one that knocks on the newsprint,
breaking the fourth wall from the other side.

Lost in the Realm of the Senses

Walking the fine line, she was always out
to find the purple, the smoke and vortex whorl.
A telephone secret, she told me one 2AM, whispered,
poured into my ear her leaden confessions.

"I've tied a silk scarf around my throat
and pulled it so tight that I nearly passed out.
The colors. I couldn't believe the lights,
the television snow and stairwell tumble."

"After that, I moved on to Tim and acid…
sucked down that tiny dot, that cartoon figure
chemical wizard. We'd go to Shoney's and order food,
just to see if we could keep the waitress from
        melting away."

"I learned about sex three joints down on a long,
smoky night. His kisses tasted of hash and ashes.
And when I woke up the next morning, I wondered
        in the mirror
whether I'd gone down on a man or a candle,
        all cold fire."

"Two years now, and I can't do two plus two.
I've fucked up good, and the colors are gone, not even
a damned scarf left to wrap around my neck.
Tim's managing the hardware section at Sears. I type and
        answer the phone."

"I'd like to have kids, but my chromosomes are no doubt
like leftover spaghetti, tangles of knotted twine.
I think of it. I dream of giving birth, but what comes out
is pure color — the color of scarves, rolling papers,
    bloodshot eyes."

"I'm past the point of strangulation, you know.
    Too natural.
What I dream of now, soaking in the tub, up to my
    tits in Calgon,
is to go that Japanese film one better, to cut off Tim's cock
while it's still in me, to see if it'll work its way to my heart."

"Like a needle."

Blessed Are the Pure of Heart:
They Have God's 800-Number

Brother Bob got back a prophylactic
in last Sunday's "pass the plate"—
a smallish square of brittle foil,
blue in a pond of pearly pink
offertory folders, stuffed and sealed.
Sister found it and fished it from the filthy lucre —
like a relic, like Alka-Seltzer, like a Twinkie
swimmin' in amongst the penny loaves.

"Visi-TA-shun, Sister! I have SEEN the future,
and it is *filled* with rubbery, demonic devil-sheaths.
Satan's fightin', *fightin'* God's cleansin' disease."

When later we come to call,
pull back your oily cheesecloth,
cheesy old oilcloth curtains,
we find you lolling in the church secretarial pool,
playing "hide the psalter," shame on you!

Give us the flea without religion.
Give us a bedbug with no grander scheme.

Oral Roberts raised Elvis Presley
on the TV late last night.

Passing for Adulthood
1986 to 2014

Never the Likes of You

I've had tea with Judge Crater
and watched buttered scones
disappear like pipe dreams in a March wind.

I've crawled on all fours with Bassett Hounds,
nose to ground, tail wagging corybantic,
found my favorite pen beneath a comfy chair.

I've seen fish fly and birds caterwaul on telephone lines.
I've been present when a tree in the forest
applauded with one hand.

I've taken Doan's Pills, 'cause I thought it was
the only game in town.

I've seen too many things to overlook you:
bathed in jam, standing in a smile,
guilty as the day the goldfish died.

Relativity

Five A.M., and the cat on my pillow
is not my cat. The pillow is not my pillow.
I've awakened in a room I do not know,
palm on breast, no movement or…

We know what it is to fall —
we dream of it, the giddy tumble
and anticipation of ground
rushing up the way a camera zooms.

But what of years' gradual descent,
our easing into love, toe first,
testing the water, then gliding in,
the way a keel cuts the wake, razor clean?

Without a frame of reference, all is still,
and I don't know where we are, tracing
flesh's blue-veined paths, heart to hand.
The touch is familiar. The cat is you.

Zen and the Art of Paper Folding

We follow the crispness of form,
all grins gone, origami to orgasm,
cosmology revealed in the crease,
or so the process goes, building
a flower, dove, white stork
posted on spindly legs,
legs like neither of us have, gladly
wrapped together like caning — blessed
by the grace of stone, purity of air.

We talk the language of our tongues.
We talk, folding it all away.

So much more than tab A in slot B.
I've seen a waterfall, a piece of paper
made into the simple life —
one that turns in to kiss itself
and marvels at its own good taste.
What you are thinking of is that stork.
Its legs are pillars; its beak
a pencil, sketching nudes.
The way to its temple
is a fine black line tucked beneath
a laughing blue brook.

The stork tells our fortune.
It catches cooties. It abides.

Juliet: the Baby Blues

We decided to wait
and that is what we do.
You and I wait for that next step.
We sit. We bide our time.
We have put that part of life on hold
and now our gonads are in a purgatory
of our own best intentions.
My sperm plays Crazy Eights.
Your eggs knit tea cozies and tiny socks.

What they never told you
was that you would be surrounded
by all these other women your age
whose coins flipped heads instead of tails.
And it hurts. The choice pummels you.
You can barely leave the house now.
Each trip to Target is an attack.
Flocks of Graco strollers circle us
like chubby buzzards on wheels.
You smile at the young mothers.
At me, later? Not so much.

Who am I kidding?
There is no poetry in each barren accusation,
no plea in a backwards glance, thinly disguised.
Instead we have your jagged sighs
at each maudlin 30-second TV spot
where baby and mother swim in yellow light,
smile, burp, bond.

On we go. We wait.
Just one more year. We wait.
Parenthood is not for us. We wait.
We will wait until we are ready —
after this limbo, this gamble
buried beneath the plans, the seeds,
the ideas gilded in words,
or stymied by rubber and Nonoxynol-9.
The mansions of what we dream
have rooms to let.
Every look you try to hide
is a "Vacancy" sign.

Brighton, MA
March, 1991

Losing My Wife (The Hair)

i.
Years ago, before the Brazilian wax
and the peer-pressured shaves of less-is-more,
this was a thing not even seen in porn:

the bare-naked pudendum — a thing of myth.
We boys imagined sliding off panties, finding it
bald, open, nothing hidden. We itched to see that day.

ii.
But now, her lack of hair creeped me out. Go figure.
The smooth skin below her navel continued
down and under and between. Just so. On and on.

There was no stubble because there was no hair.
Not a single lone strand, fine or thick,
straight or twisted like familiar black commas.

It was all missing as if it had never existed.
All gone without waxing or shaving. No plucking
or pruning. She hadn't Epilady-ed 'til she screamed.

It never grew because it had never grown.
Here she was at age 30, pretending to age backwards,
first smooth as a peach, now seemingly without fuzz.

iii.
Two months plus one week out of chemo,
she still exhaled chemicals, peed chemicals.
I closed my eyes in our darkened bedroom

and it was chemicals that scratched my back
with the rusted iron of ghost needles,
pinched me bloody for spite and "fair is fair."

When my tongue touched any part of her,
she tasted no more like herself than epoxy.
She tasted of ifosfamide and fear.

iv.
When the hair grew back, coarse and strong,
it curled the other way like the drain
in a different hemisphere. A drain without water,

a once-open something since sealed shut.
Everything closed. Everything stayed closed.
The reborn hair? A seed coat, a hymen, a shell.

Mixture

Irish Jay and Nick the Greek, bellies to the bar rail,
one eye each on Rocket's stretch,
pitch, swing — in here, all sides retired.
They say I'm young; I'd say I'm damned for middle age.
"Yer too young to remember the A-line on Brighton Ave
or the Not-So-Great Fire of '39, famous if only
for its means of being doused —
the hoors of Black Pete's Alley what some says
married rich." They forget her face, but
they still toast Galen with the third nipple,
a marvel to behold by the light of dime store candles.
"She was a good woman, God bless her, sober or drunk."

I walked home the old long way, past Saint E's
high on the hill, filled with its antiseptic rooms
and weepy statues of Mary and those tunnels
through the mountain with its white neon cross.
That was my shortcut, that is how I would go,
through those basement halls lined with laundry carts,
past Jesus's ATM, a right, left, then right…
in on Cambridge Street and out on Washington,
then jaywalk like a boss across to Steve's Pizza.
Steve was Greek, like Nick, and always knew us
when we called for take-out — pizza and salad.
Juliet was no Galen, but she always made Steve laugh.

In those slow beige years before everyone died —
Juliet, my grandmother, my father —
Steve sold his store and moved to Cyprus.

70

A Hood truck hurrying to stock a school,
a thousand cartons of milk and tiny ice creams,
carried more than enough momentum
to crumple Nick like an empty pack of Salems.
Eventually, even the A-line tracks sensed
the end was near and buckled a wave good-bye.
Nothing could keep them down. Not a cold rain
or the empty promises of progress or the sighs
of the replacement 57 Bus, dodging steel.

It's not that these stories connect. They don't.
They're more a dry mixture, something that
can be separated by the right combination
of sifting, dissolving, attempts to float or sink.

The unrehearsed toast teeters between wake
and wedding reception, undecided in the moment
whether the joke is appropriate,
whether the guests are ghosts intent
on sucking dry the rented champagne fountain,
whether the couple leaving in the parked limo
is heading for a honeymoon or Eternal Peace.
The driver won't tell. The toast begins
and I look for you. All of you.
The imagined barfly no less than the wife...
sharing the best wishes, the hope
that all of this goes on.

Acceleration Due to Gravity

Hang on then.
Hang on tight to wonder
and the wide-eyed,
interpersonal, adrenalin rush
of meeting and falling.
tumbling down the rabbit hole
together.

Cling to the heart skip,
the search for the right word
and the fumbling delights
of kisses quick and tentative,
and kisses long, sweet, and new.

Is anything really that color?
Can anything really be as soft
as that skin under there
or this skin…?
This skin? This skin here and here?

What happens if I…?
What happens when you…?

Tumbling together in the dark,
we make distant breathless beginnings
linger and loll.
Let them slip like silk
sliding down a shaved thigh.

Step barefoot from damp panties
and blush like the first time
you were caught looking…
or you invited someone to look.

Our hearts are in our hands.
We offer; we accept;
we fondle, squeeze, pinch, lick,
caress, nuzzle with a gentle hum
and try hard not to spindle, not to hurt.

Hang on then.
Together we fall.

And space…?
Space isn't empty.
And time isn't scary.
And love is the curve of that time,
cupped in my hand,
warm and exciting…

So what if we never land?

Love Like That (for Amy)

Love's like toast and jam.
Love's like sweet chocolate.
Love's like memory and wishes —
like our past and present
slow dancing together,
bare feet on the worn midnight rug,
lights out and kids asleep.
It's like a goodnight kiss
with eyes open.

Love's like our fingers interlocked,
linked side by side by side
as we walk down the street
hand in hand at sunset,
or later in bed,
straining
to keep the one on top
from melting with joy,
aching
to keep the one on the bottom
from flying away.

The Tug between Two Masses

Leap to me. Close your fine eyes.
Think of my soft lips
brushing your neck, my hands
firm at your waist.

Take a breath, steady your resolve...
and step out in the blackness.
Be that pebble waiting to drop
into the still waters
of a sleeping lake.

Become the wind
rushing in your own hair.

As you fall, fall into the promise
of light, of my waiting touch,
fall feeling gravity's path
and life's wanton promises.

You are a flower petal
and you are a rocket.

I will catch you.
I will catch you.

Waltz

There is no seven-year itch.
There is only the long march.

How do we continue to walk
side by side
when my legs grow longer, day by day?
Even if we synchronize
(I shorten my stride,
you pick up your pace),
what of the accidental disharmony —
a life-weary stumble,
an exuberant skipped step —
that leaves us hitched up
and awkwardly adjusting?
Who runs to catch up?
Who waits at the corner?

What I don't know won't hurt me.
I sit on the bench, knowing you
are less than a block away
and that you will always come…
unless you're sitting on another bench,
waiting for me.

We should probably buy a treadmill.

Blink Once and You're Gone

Perhaps it's a myopic conclusion.
But memories of my life in sex
seem best approached
sideways and nonchalant.
To me, they only appear in focus
when I look at them askance,
almost from the corner of my eye.
It's like trying to catch sight
of the Pleiades head on,
the particulars only fade when faced down.

For the most part, I remember the facts.
My first orgasm is the stuff of myth —
all epic and embellished in the retelling.
Perhaps the facts of that late night episode aren't facts.
Perhaps *The Odyssey* wasn't as grand as all that
and my own sticky scared confused joy of an instant
was less than I think, more than I know.

I know the first breast I bussed.
I remember the song that was playing
when she pulled off her rib knit top.
I can easily picture her pale pink nipples
and the gaudy plaid of her parents' couch.
But, beyond that, there on the tip of a smile,
both skin and cloth quickly fade into a ball of fuzz,
hidden in Taurus, a smudge of light
like the poignant snort of a bull.

Even the first pussy I poked
is lost in a nebula of subsequent history —
whisky of the dueling seduction,
the big bang of unintended disdain,
explosive distance and then our eventual reconstitution
as old friends. (I must admit,
there are several stars in *that* constellation.)

You see, while I know it takes 440 years
for light to travel from the Pleiades
just to play tricks on my eyes,
I can only suspect that the distance
between my heart and my brain,
between my cock and my memory,
is far less… yet also far less direct.

And while I can't quite see them,
I know that around those stars dance
a host of nearly invisible suitors,
a hundred beaus for each of Seven Sisters,
a thousand kisses for each beau,
a million ways that each time I push into you
and hear you sigh and let go
it is both old and new.
In semi-darkness and without my glasses,
I see what I don't see:
bottle of lube, pack o' pills,
candle, book, sheen of sweat,
hair falling across your face;

our fingers, white-knuckled, entwined;
the dent of my weight
pushing your wrists into the mattress.

Which way do I look
to see the memory beginning?
Which way do I look
to keep from seeing it end?

Genealogy

Maternal
When I tried to show my mother
our family tree, she wouldn't even look.
She gave me the smoothest of old lady shuffles,
a skill passed from generation to generation.
"Can you get me some ice chips?"
This was her geriatric way of saying,
"Look! It's Halley's comet!"
and slowly bolting for the door.

I wanted to show her how far back I'd gone,
to see the names, the dates, the ascent of lines.
I wanted to hear her tell me stories.
Instead she fiddled with her oxygen
and asked if I could please adjust the blinds.
She was almost as boldly evasive
as that time when I asked her at age 12
why she'd never wanted kids.

On the one hand, I get it. I do.
She didn't want to see her name there
on my tablet, me flipping pages into the past.
She really couldn't look at her box
with its "to be decided" missing date.
Like a headstone with a name
and no date of death — it waits,
knowing better than you of inevitability.

Paternal
My father never had that problem.
Not with technology, not with the tree
and its branches with their dead leaves
or all those leaves like his leaf,
the ones in the process of turning —
flaming out to red, mellowing to gold,
sighing their way to brown.
To him, anything past 70 was gravy.

And that man was all about the stories,
even if half weren't true (more than half
if my grandfather or his dad told it first).
When he sold the business, my father
kept the clock from the general store —
20 years his elder, if not more. He seemed
to appreciate how things wind down.
And then — to prove it — he did.

Internal
Here's my leaf — another box with a date
to be filled in later by someone not me.
It's a box with no category for colonoscopies.
There are no stories of Cialis and cholesterol.
(When did the upkeep of an aging human
become more complex than sitting still?)
The stories are footnotes, crossing lines.
I have the family clock. I wind it. It ticks.
With or without me, it will be spring again.

About the Poet

Andrew Amster was born and raised in Lexington, Kentucky. He was accepted into a creative writing program as a college freshman. This was clearly ridiculous since he had yet to do anything in his life and therefore had nothing to write about. To quote his professors, his poems were "didactic" and his short stories "melodramatic horseshit." Since then, he has been a geologist, a teacher, a writer/editor of assorted science educational doodads, and has seen years do what years do. He is the father of two, the husband of one, and is unapologetic for any poem he may have happened to write about a supercontinent.

www.ingramcontent.com/pod-product-compliance
Lightning Source LLC
Chambersburg PA
CBHW032113040426
42337CB00040B/396